The Dua Journal

Copyright © 2018 The Dua Journal. All rights reserved.

Created by Umeda Islamova
Printed in U.S.

No part of this publication may be reproduced, or stored in a retrieval system, or transmitted in any form or by any means, electronic, mechanical, recording, photocopying, scanning, or otherwise, without express written permission of the publisher.

For information about permission to reproduce selections from this book, email salaam@theduajournal.com.

Visit our web site at www.theduajournal.com.

PUBLISHER'S DISCLAIMER

While the author has used best efforts in preparing this book, she makes no representations or warranties with respect to the accuracy or completeness of the content of this book. Neither the publisher nor author shall be liable for any loss of profit or any other commercial damages, including but not limited to special, incidental, consequential or other damages.

ISBN: 978-0-692-07905-8
FIRST EDITION

DEDICATION

For the little heart that yearns for the big love.

INTRODUCTION

In the name of Allah, the Most Merciful, the Most Kind.

Salam! My name is Umeda. I want to tell you a story. When I was little, I used to go to Sunday School where I was taught about Allah, Islam, Prophet Muhammad, and being a good Muslim.

I learned a lot about what I needed to do and how I needed to behave to be a good Muslim. But one thing I didn't learn was how to feel close to Allah.

I thought about Allah, but it was mostly when I was upset or when I really needed something. Behaving towards Allah like this seemed fine until I got older. Then I experienced my friends and family who would only call me or be with me when they were upset or wanted something. It didn't feel good. I wanted my friends and family to want to be with me even when they didn't need something from me.

But then, I remembered that's exactly what I did to Allah. I love Allah and to make my choices show that I loved him, I needed to change something. So I started talking to Allah more. Inside my head and inside my heart. I silently started talking to him.

When something made me smile, silently I said, "Allah, thank you for this moment. That made me feel very nice. I know this only happened because you wanted to gift me this good feeling."

And then when I ate something and wasn't hungry anymore, I silently said, "Thank you for this clean, safe, and good food." Or if I get confused, I would ask Allah to help me figure it out. I asked Allah to show me the answers and to help me understand.

Of course, I didn't talk to Allah every second of my day. I would get focused on the different activities I did day to day. I would get busy. But every time I remembered, I would talk to Allah.

The funny thing is, the more I spoke to Allah, the more I remembered Allah. The more I remembered Allah, the more things and people reminded me of Allah.

The more I asked something from Allah, the more they were answered. It felt good to get the things I was asking for just days or weeks ago.

I felt closer to Allah, as if He was right there with me at all times. That feeling brought me peace and happiness. I haven't felt alone again. I challenge you to bring in Allah in everything you do as well. See how that makes you feel.

I created The Dua Journal to help you remember Allah and to be a happy Muslim. It gives you inspiration on making your own duas. It gives you space to think about all the gifts Allah blesses you with. And it helps you set goals to actively work on being an even better Muslim.

Now, I will tell you more about each section.

The Prophet ﷺ said:

"Whoever wishes that Allah responds to his dua in times of hardship, then let him increase his dua in times of ease."

al-Tirmidhi 3382

I make dua for...

There are duas that come from the Quran, some from our Prophet Muhammad ﷺ, but we can also make our own dua. Dua is a conversation with Allah. It is a way for us to call on Him at any time, any place, and in any situation. Dua is a wonderful way to bring Allah to our everyday life. As we get in a habit of making dua, Allah becomes more significant in our thoughts and day to day experiences.

Through dua, we are reminded that He listens to us at all times, He hears our thoughts, and He is the source of all our hopes. Making dua also reminds us that we depend on Allah for everything in this life. Whatever comforts we have today, they are all from Allah. Knowing this is the root of being a Muslim.

Here are a few things to remember when making dua:

Make dua at all times. Dua is a conversation with Allah, and you should have it regularly, outside of your prayers and this journal, even when you feel joyful and at peace. Get in the habit of consciously monitoring your thoughts and involving Allah in them.

Make dua for all matters. Nothing is too small to ask Allah, and nothing is impossible for Him. Even the smallest action cannot happen unless Allah wills it, and His will can heal even the worst of situations.

Make dua with good intentions. Avoid asking for things that will cause harm. Focus on positivity, kindness, and mercy.

Make dua for matters of this world and the hereafter. There must be a balance between the two. Think both short- and long-term when making your duas.

Make dua for yourself first. Then make dua for your loved ones, the Prophet ﷺ, and the community as a whole. Prophet Muhammad ﷺ would often start his dua with himself first. Avoid getting in the habit of asking others to make dua for you and failing to do one for yourself.

Make dua earnestly. Ask from the bottom of your heart. Really want what you are asking for. Be insistent, sincere, and humble, and imagine having your duas answered.

Make dua with an expectation that Allah will respond to it. Expect only the best from Allah. All things are possible and available with Him. Be confident that Allah will hear you and respond.

Make dua even when they are not answered quickly. Don't be discouraged when Allah delays His response. Be patient and keep making dua.

Make dua and set goals towards achieving them. Choose to work with Allah. Don't expect Him to do all the work. Think of things you can do to achieve your duas and do them.

Islam goals I am working on are...

As a Muslim, it is very important for us to learn, learn, learn. Allah gave us a lot of interesting things to learn, and we can't really be done with learning. Even when you are much older, you will still be learning about Islam. The way to be a successful Muslim is to stay curious and to set little goals to keep learning.

Your goals are completely up to you. Maybe you will set your own goals or maybe you will pick goals with your parent or teacher. Goals can be memorizing a surah, not talking back to your parents, learning Arabic, learning how to pray, reading Quran, reading an Islamic book, learning about the Prophet, going to Sunday School, etc.

Once you choose a goal, you keep writing your goal until you meet it. For example, if your Islam goal is memorizing Surah Al-Fatiha, you keep writing it down until you have memorized the surah. Then you move on to the next goal. And yes, of course, you can have more than one goal.

One goal could be about education like *memorizing a surah* and your other goal could be about character like *not fighting with a sibling*.

Never stop setting goals to be an even better Muslim. Always grow.

One thing I wish I did differently...

There is always room for improvement. This is the space for you to reflect on your behavior and choices.

Was there a choice you weren't the most proud of today? Was there a time when you could have done a better job of something? Were you your best self today? Was there a situation which you could have handled better? Was there a person you could have treated better?

Often, we can control how the day turns out by the way we *respond* to different situations.

Do notice the wording: even better. Every day is a good day. Every day that you are breathing is a gift from Allah. Every event that you go through is either a blessing or a lesson.

Today's happy moments were:

This is a place to capture positive, joyful moments in your daily life. When you fill out this section, you automatically replay the day's events. It's a joyful experience to think about all the good things that happened.

A happy life is made up of a bunch of little happy moments. So gather all your happy moments here every day.

On the days you are needing a reminder of how blessed you are, go back and read the happy moments from past days.

"Be thankful to Allah: whoever gives thanks benefits his own soul, and as for those who are thankless–Allah is self-sufficient, worthy of all praise."

Quran 31:12

I am grateful for...

Gratitude can be for people, things, events, circumstances, etc. Gratitude isn't just words. It's a habit of paying attention to the gifts of Allah and thanking Him for choosing to give those gifts to us. It's an exercise of putting greater value on people, things, events, etc. through imagining life without them. Gratitude is acknowledging that those things didn't have to happen or didn't have to be given to us, but because they were, we've gained in some way. Most importantly, gratitude is tracing our blessings back to where they came from, from Allah.

Here are a few points about gratitude:

Gratitude makes you humble. Each of us is blessed in so many ways, most of which we don't pay attention to. Through gratitude, we realize that we did not earn any of our blessings. Allah chose to gift each of our blessings specifically to us.

Gratitude opens your eyes to your gifts. What if we made a conscious choice to take nothing in our lives for granted, not even the simplest blessings – breathing, our senses, mobility, speech, family, etc.? The more blessings you open your eyes to, the more you will see.

Gratitude increases your patience. It gives us something to hold on to until situations unfold in their proper times.

Gratitude helps you enjoy the now. Our human nature constantly wants more. Gratitude focuses us on what we *have* by removing the distractions of what we *want.*

Gratitude helps you recognize the kindness of others. Allah asks us to be grateful to those around us and to return their favors. Imagine how much better the world would be if people made the choice to make each other happy.

Gratitude increases Allah's blessings upon you. In Surah Ibrahim [14:7], Allah states: "And remember when your Lord proclaimed, 'If you are grateful, I will surely increase you in favor.'"

Gratitude interrupts anxiety, worries, and stress. Practicing gratitude puts our minds on positive things, builds a trusting and loving relationship with Allah, and gives us an understanding that our needs are already being met. Combined, these outcomes keep us away from unproductive, negative emotions.

Gratitude brings contentment. Many scientific studies show that regular practice of gratitude improves physical, mental, and emotional well-being. Gratitude has also been shown to increase positive emotions and improve relationships.

Today I learned...

I already mentioned the importance of learning as a Muslim. This is a place you can put down a few things you learned. It doesn't have to be something big. It can be as small as learning something about yourself or others or it can be what you learned from a story you read, listened to, or watched. It could be from the Quran. Whatever you learn, always remember to focus on learning things that will help you grow, not things that just waste your time.

A note on consistency:

Reading the benefits of dua, gratitude, and reflection are motivating, but it can be difficult to maintain them as regular practices. To reap full benefits, these activities need to be established into habits.

The easiest way to form a habit is to find something you *already do consistently*, and follow it with The Dua Journal. For example, brushing your teeth, doing homework, eating dinner, etc. As soon as you are done with it, grab your journal and find a comfortable place to reflect.

You will need to be your own cheerleader and push yourself to come back to the journal. It only takes a few minutes. Have fun with it!

Now it's time to begin your new journey. Start by making an intention. What do you want to gain from filling out this journal? What do you think it will help you with? How will you be different at the end?

_____

_____

_____

_____

_____

DATE ___/___/___

Allah, I know you can hear me at all times and know the truth at all times, so protect me from telling lies.

I make dua for...

_____
_____
_____
_____

Islam goals I am working on are...

_____
_____
_____
_____

One thing I wish I did differently to make today even better was...

_____
_____
_____
_____

Today's happy moments were...

I am grateful for...

Today I learned...

DATE ___/___/___

Allah, make my life joyful and fill me
with gratitude for your blessings.

I make dua for...

_____
_____
_____
_____

Islam goals I am working on are...

_____
_____
_____
_____

One thing I wish I did differently to make today even better was...

_____
_____
_____

Today's happy moments were...

I am grateful for...

Today I learned...

DATE ___/___/___

Allah, increase my curiosity and interest in things that are good for me.

I make dua for...

_____
_____
_____
_____

Islam goals I am working on are...

_____
_____
_____
_____

One thing I wish I did differently to make today even better was...

_____
_____
_____

Today's happy moments were...

I am grateful for...

Today I learned...

DATE ___/___/___

Allah, forgive me for the bad choices I made knowingly and unknowingly.

I make dua for...

_____
_____
_____
_____

Islam goals I am working on are...

_____
_____
_____
_____

One thing I wish I did differently to make today even better was...

_____
_____
_____

Today's happy moments were...

I am grateful for...

Today I learned...

DATE ___/___/___

Allah, fill me with peace and patience when I'm going through a difficult time.

I make dua for...

_____
_____
_____
_____

Islam goals I am working on are...

_____
_____
_____
_____

One thing I wish I did differently to make today even better was...

_____
_____
_____

Today's happy moments were...

I am grateful for...

Today I learned...

DATE ___/___/___

Allah, be with me and guide me through all my feelings. Help me remember that all my feelings will come and go and that You will always remain.

I make dua for...

_____
_____
_____
_____

Islam goals I am working on are...

_____
_____
_____
_____

One thing I wish I did differently to make today even better was...

_____
_____
_____

Today's happy moments were...

I am grateful for...

Today I learned...

DATE ___/___/___

Allah, You gifted this body to me. Help me take good care of it by eating healthy and being active.

I make dua for...

_____
_____
_____
_____

Islam goals I am working on are...

_____
_____
_____
_____

One thing I wish I did differently to make today even better was...

_____
_____
_____

Today's happy moments were...

I am grateful for...

Today I learned...

DATE ___/___/___

Allah, give me motivation to learn about Your religion, Your Book, and Your Prophet.

I make dua for...

___
___
___
___

Islam goals I am working on are...

___
___
___
___

One thing I wish I did differently to make today even better was...

___
___
___

Today's happy moments were...

I am grateful for...

Today I learned...

DATE ___/___/___

Allah, make me one who trusts You completely when it comes to things I cannot control.

I make dua for...

_____
_____
_____
_____

Islam goals I am working on are...

_____
_____
_____
_____

One thing I wish I did differently to make today even better was...

_____
_____
_____

Today's happy moments were...

I am grateful for...

Today I learned...

DATE ___/___/___

Allah, I ask You for protection from everything that is bad.

I make dua for...

_____
_____
_____
_____

Islam goals I am working on are...

_____
_____
_____
_____

One thing I wish I did differently to make today even better was...

_____
_____
_____
_____

Today's happy moments were...

I am grateful for...

Today I learned...

DATE ___/___/___

Allah, I ask You for peace in my home,
in my city, in my country, and in the world.

I make dua for...

_____
_____
_____
_____

Islam goals I am working on are...

_____
_____
_____
_____

One thing I wish I did differently to make today even better was...

_____
_____
_____

Today's happy moments were...

I am grateful for...

Today I learned...

DATE ___/___/___

Allah, help me memorize and understand the Quran with ease.

I make dua for...

___

___

___

___

Islam goals I am working on are...

___

___

___

___

One thing I wish I did differently to make today even better was...

___

___

___

Today's happy moments were...

I am grateful for...

Today I learned...

DATE ___/___/___

Allah, help me balance my time between all my activities. Protect me from spending too much time on any one thing, especially when it is not beneficial for me.

I make dua for…

_____
_____
_____
_____

Islam goals I am working on are…

_____
_____
_____
_____

One thing I wish I did differently to make today even better was…

_____
_____
_____

Today's happy moments were...

I am grateful for...

Today I learned...

DATE ___/___/___

Allah, make it easy for me to follow my parents' directions.

I make dua for...

___

Islam goals I am working on are...

___

One thing I wish I did differently to make today even better was...

Today's happy moments were...

I am grateful for...

Today I learned...

DATE ___/___/___

Allah, bless my parents with health and happiness.

I make dua for...

_____
_____
_____
_____

Islam goals I am working on are...

_____
_____
_____
_____

One thing I wish I did differently to make today even better was...

_____
_____
_____

Today's happy moments were...

I am grateful for...

Today I learned...

DATE ___/___/___

Allah, guide me and my family to the right path, the path that will bring us closer to You.

I make dua for...

_____
_____
_____
_____

Islam goals I am working on are...

_____
_____
_____
_____

One thing I wish I did differently to make today even better was...

_____
_____
_____
_____

Today's happy moments were...

I am grateful for...

Today I learned...

DATE ___/___/___

Allah, I ask You for good dreams
and protection from bad dreams.

I make dua for...

_____
_____
_____
_____
_____

Islam goals I am working on are...

_____
_____
_____
_____

One thing I wish I did differently to make today even better was...

_____
_____
_____

Today's happy moments were...

I am grateful for...

Today I learned...

DATE ___/___/___

Allah, keep me away from people who will push me to do things You won't be proud of.

I make dua for...

_____
_____
_____
_____

Islam goals I am working on are...

_____
_____
_____
_____

One thing I wish I did differently to make today even better was...

_____
_____
_____

Today's happy moments were...

I am grateful for...

Today I learned...

DATE ___/___/___

Allah, help me save my money and when I do spend it, help me spend it wisely.

I make dua for...

_____
_____
_____
_____

Islam goals I am working on are...

_____
_____
_____
_____

One thing I wish I did differently to make today even better was...

_____
_____
_____

Today's happy moments were...

I am grateful for...

Today I learned...

DATE ___/___/___

Allah, make me a likeable person and bless me with many good friends.

I make dua for...

_____
_____
_____
_____

Islam goals I am working on are...

_____
_____
_____
_____

One thing I wish I did differently to make today even better was...

_____
_____
_____

Today's happy moments were...

I am grateful for...

Today I learned...

DATE ___/___/___

Allah, make me one who values your blessings. Make me one who treats everyone and everything with kindness and respect.

I make dua for...

_____
_____
_____
_____

Islam goals I am working on are...

_____
_____
_____
_____

One thing I wish I did differently to make today even better was...

_____
_____
_____

Today's happy moments were...

I am grateful for...

Today I learned...

DATE ___/___/___

Allah, make me brave and help me overcome my fears.

I make dua for...

_____
_____
_____
_____

Islam goals I am working on are...

_____
_____
_____

One thing I wish I did differently to make today even better was...

_____
_____
_____

Today's happy moments were...

I am grateful for...

Today I learned...

DATE ___/___/___

Allah, help me understand and explain
my feelings more clearly.

I make dua for...

_____
_____
_____
_____
_____

Islam goals I am working on are...

_____
_____
_____
_____

One thing I wish I did differently to make today even better was...

_____
_____
_____
_____

Today's happy moments were...

I am grateful for...

Today I learned...

DATE ___/___/___

Allah, guide me towards the answers
when I am feeling confused.

I make dua for...

_____
_____
_____
_____

Islam goals I am working on are...

_____
_____
_____
_____

One thing I wish I did differently to make today even better was...

_____
_____
_____

Today's happy moments were...

I am grateful for...

Today I learned...

DATE ___/___/___

Allah, protect me from saying bad words
and doing bad things to other people.

I make dua for...

_____
_____
_____
_____

Islam goals I am working on are...

_____
_____
_____
_____

One thing I wish I did differently to make today even better was...

_____
_____
_____

Today's happy moments were...

I am grateful for...

Today I learned...

DATE ___/___/___

Allah, what You think of me is more important to me. Protect me from worrying too much about what others think of me.

I make dua for...

_____
_____
_____
_____

Islam goals I am working on are...

_____
_____
_____
_____

One thing I wish I did differently to make today even better was...

_____
_____
_____

Today's happy moments were...

I am grateful for...

Today I learned...

DATE ___/___/___

Allah, make me a forgiving person and don't let me hold a grudge against anybody.

I make dua for...

_____
_____
_____
_____

Islam goals I am working on are...

_____
_____
_____
_____

One thing I wish I did differently to make today even better was...

_____
_____
_____

Today's happy moments were...

| |
| |

I am grateful for...

| |
| |

Today I learned...

| |
| |

DATE ___/___/___

Allah, I pray that everything that happens to me will make me grow to be who You want me to be.

I make dua for...

_____
_____
_____
_____

Islam goals I am working on are...

_____
_____
_____
_____

One thing I wish I did differently to make today even better was...

_____
_____
_____
_____

Today's happy moments were...

I am grateful for...

Today I learned...

DATE ___/___/___

Allah, make me a kind and caring person.
Make it easy for me to think about others before myself.

I make dua for...

_____
_____
_____
_____
_____

Islam goals I am working on are...

_____
_____
_____
_____
_____

One thing I wish I did differently to make today even better was...

_____
_____
_____
_____

Today's happy moments were...

I am grateful for...

Today I learned...

DATE ___/___/___

Allah, guide me to ways I can better myself and make it easy for me to learn new skills.

I make dua for...

_____
_____
_____
_____

Islam goals I am working on are...

_____
_____
_____
_____

One thing I wish I did differently to make today even better was...

_____
_____
_____
_____

Today's happy moments were...

I am grateful for...

Today I learned...

DATE ___/___/___

Allah, bless my teachers with kind hearts and understanding.

I make dua for...

_____
_____
_____
_____

Islam goals I am working on are...

_____
_____
_____
_____

One thing I wish I did differently to make today even better was...

_____
_____
_____

Today's happy moments were...

I am grateful for...

Today I learned...

DATE ___/___/___

Allah, protect me from wild animals, from drowning, from getting burnt, and from falling and hurting myself.

I make dua for...

_____
_____
_____
_____

Islam goals I am working on are...

_____
_____
_____
_____

One thing I wish I did differently to make today even better was...

_____
_____
_____
_____

Today's happy moments were...

I am grateful for...

Today I learned...

DATE ___/___/___

Allah, gift me with clothes, things, and foods I enjoy.

I make dua for...

_____
_____
_____
_____

Islam goals I am working on are...

_____
_____
_____
_____

One thing I wish I did differently to make today even better was...

_____
_____
_____
_____

Today's happy moments were...

I am grateful for...

Today I learned...

DATE ___/___/___

Allah, cleanse my heart from any bad feelings.
Cleanse my mind from bad thoughts.

I make dua for...

_____
_____
_____
_____
_____

Islam goals I am working on are...

_____
_____
_____
_____

One thing I wish I did differently to make today even better was...

_____
_____
_____

Today's happy moments were...

I am grateful for...

Today I learned...

DATE ___/___/___

Allah, help me master the skills to calm myself down when I am frustrated and angry.

I make dua for...

_____
_____
_____
_____

Islam goals I am working on are...

_____
_____
_____
_____

One thing I wish I did differently to make today even better was...

_____
_____
_____

Today's happy moments were...

I am grateful for...

Today I learned...

DATE ___/___/___

Allah, I know You can do even the impossible if You will. Make me one who trusts You completely.

I make dua for...

_____
_____
_____
_____

Islam goals I am working on are...

_____
_____
_____
_____

One thing I wish I did differently to make today even better was...

_____
_____
_____

Today's happy moments were...

I am grateful for...

Today I learned...

DATE ___/___/___

Allah, grow my love both for You and Your Prophet, Muhammad ﷺ عليه وسلم.

I make dua for...

_____
_____
_____
_____

Islam goals I am working on are...

_____
_____
_____
_____

One thing I wish I did differently to make today even better was...

_____
_____
_____

Today's happy moments were...

I am grateful for...

Today I learned...

DATE ___/___/___

Allah, give me the motivation to do my prayers on time, now and when I grow up.

I make dua for...

_____
_____
_____
_____

Islam goals I am working on are...

_____
_____
_____
_____

One thing I wish I did differently to make today even better was...

_____
_____
_____

Today's happy moments were...

I am grateful for...

Today I learned...

DATE ___/___/___

Allah, make me a good and respectful student.

I make dua for...

_____
_____
_____
_____

Islam goals I am working on are...

_____
_____
_____
_____

One thing I wish I did differently to make today even better was...

_____
_____
_____

Today's happy moments were...

I am grateful for...

Today I learned...

DATE ___/___/___

Allah, give me the opportunity to learn all
Your names and help me live by those qualities.

I make dua for...

_____
_____
_____
_____

Islam goals I am working on are...

_____
_____
_____
_____

One thing I wish I did differently to make today even better was...

_____
_____
_____
_____

Today's happy moments were...

I am grateful for...

Today I learned...

DATE ___/___/___

Allah, answer my duas and the duas of my family and friends.

I make dua for...

_____
_____
_____
_____

Islam goals I am working on are...

_____
_____
_____
_____

One thing I wish I did differently to make today even better was...

_____
_____
_____
_____

Today's happy moments were...

I am grateful for...

Today I learned...

DATE ___/___/___

Allah, help me trust that the bad events in my life are my tests and not my punishments. I ask that I learn from both good and bad events and that I trust You to get me through. I make dua for...

_____
_____
_____
_____

Islam goals I am working on are...

_____
_____
_____
_____

One thing I wish I did differently to make today even better was...

_____
_____
_____
_____

Today's happy moments were...

I am grateful for...

Today I learned...

DATE ___/___/___

Allah, I ask You to keep me away from over-eating, over-speaking, and over-spending.

I make dua for...

_____
_____
_____
_____

Islam goals I am working on are...

_____
_____
_____
_____

One thing I wish I did differently to make today even better was...

_____
_____
_____
_____

Today's happy moments were...

I am grateful for...

Today I learned...

DATE ___/___/___

Allah, surround me with people, things, and events that will make me a better Muslim.

I make dua for...

_____
_____
_____
_____
_____

Islam goals I am working on are...

_____
_____
_____
_____

One thing I wish I did differently to make today even better was...

_____
_____
_____

Today's happy moments were...

I am grateful for...

Today I learned...

DATE ___/___/___

Allah, I ask You for protection from laziness.

I make dua for...

_____
_____
_____
_____

Islam goals I am working on are...

_____
_____
_____
_____

One thing I wish I did differently to make today even better was...

_____
_____
_____
_____

Today's happy moments were...

I am grateful for...

Today I learned...

DATE ___/___/___

Allah, this is an exciting time of my life.
Make each stage of my childhood enjoyable for me.
And keep me from wanting to rush into being an adult.
I make dua for...

_____
_____
_____
_____

Islam goals I am working on are...

_____
_____
_____
_____

One thing I wish I did differently to make today even better was...

_____
_____
_____
_____

Today's happy moments were...

I am grateful for...

Today I learned...

DATE ___/___/___

Allah, protect me from hurting anyone's feelings.
And protect others from hurting my feelings.

I make dua for...

_____
_____
_____
_____

Islam goals I am working on are...

_____
_____
_____
_____

One thing I wish I did differently to make today even better was...

_____
_____
_____
_____

Today's happy moments were...

I am grateful for...

Today I learned...

DATE ___/___/___

Allah, I ask You for courage to do
the good things that seem very difficult.

I make dua for...

_____
_____
_____
_____

Islam goals I am working on are...

_____
_____
_____
_____

One thing I wish I did differently to make today even better was...

_____
_____
_____

Today's happy moments were...

I am grateful for...

Today I learned...

DATE ___/___/___

Allah, I ask You for forgiveness for the bad deeds I keep doing over and over again.

I make dua for...

_____
_____
_____
_____

Islam goals I am working on are...

_____
_____
_____
_____

One thing I wish I did differently to make today even better was...

_____
_____
_____
_____

Today's happy moments were...

I am grateful for...

Today I learned...

DATE ___/___/___

Allah, give me eyes that see the best in people, a heart that forgives the worst, a mind that forgets the bad, and a soul that never loses faith. I make dua for...

_____
_____
_____
_____

Islam goals I am working on are...

_____
_____
_____
_____

One thing I wish I did differently to make today even better was...

_____
_____
_____

Today's happy moments were...

I am grateful for...

Today I learned...

DATE ___/___/___

Allah, make my future better than my present and past.

I make dua for...

_____
_____
_____
_____

Islam goals I am working on are...

_____
_____
_____
_____

One thing I wish I did differently to make today even better was...

_____
_____
_____
_____

Today's happy moments were...

I am grateful for...

Today I learned...

DATE ___/___/___

Allah, it hurts inside to see my parents upset. Give them peace and patience and fill my heart with peace and comfort. With You everything is possible. I make dua for...

_____

_____

_____

_____

Islam goals I am working on are...

_____

_____

_____

_____

One thing I wish I did differently to make today even better was...

_____

_____

_____

_____

Today's happy moments were...

I am grateful for...

Today I learned...

DATE ___/___/___

Allah, I ask You to shield me from poverty, from hunger, from a broken heart.

I make dua for...

___
___
___
___

Islam goals I am working on are...

___
___
___
___

One thing I wish I did differently to make today even better was...

___
___
___

Today's happy moments were...

I am grateful for...

Today I learned...

DATE ___/___/___

Allah, accept and reward the good things I've done.

I make dua for...

_____
_____
_____
_____

Islam goals I am working on are...

_____
_____
_____
_____

One thing I wish I did differently to make today even better was...

_____
_____
_____

Today's happy moments were...

I am grateful for...

Today I learned...

DATE ___/___/___

Allah, I know everything I have is a gift from You and that everything can be taken away by You. Make my heart a grateful heart.
I make dua for...

_____
_____
_____
_____

Islam goals I am working on are...

_____
_____
_____
_____

One thing I wish I did differently to make today even better was...

_____
_____
_____

Today's happy moments were...

I am grateful for...

Today I learned...

DATE ___/___/___

Allah, shield me from bad people and bad events.

I make dua for...

_____
_____
_____
_____

Islam goals I am working on are...

_____
_____
_____
_____

One thing I wish I did differently to make today even better was...

_____
_____
_____
_____

Today's happy moments were...

I am grateful for...

Today I learned...

DATE ___/___/___

Allah, let me be one of the people who get to meet You in heaven one day.

I make dua for...

_____
_____
_____
_____

Islam goals I am working on are...

_____
_____
_____
_____

One thing I wish I did differently to make today even better was...

_____
_____
_____

Today's happy moments were...

I am grateful for...

Today I learned...

DATE ___/___/___

Allah, help me focus on what I am saying when I am praying and when I am reciting my surahs.

I make dua for...

_____
_____
_____
_____

Islam goals I am working on are...

_____
_____
_____
_____

One thing I wish I did differently to make today even better was...

_____
_____
_____

Today's happy moments were...

I am grateful for...

Today I learned...

DATE ___/___/___

Allah, show me ways I can make people I love happy and joyful.

I make dua for...

___

Islam goals I am working on are...

___

One thing I wish I did differently to make today even better was...

Today's happy moments were...

I am grateful for...

Today I learned...

DATE ___/___/___

Allah, protect me from deafness, blindness, and serious illnesses. Thank you for everything that works well in my body. I make dua for...

_____
_____
_____
_____

Islam goals I am working on are...

_____
_____
_____
_____

One thing I wish I did differently to make today even better was...

_____
_____
_____

Today's happy moments were...

I am grateful for...

Today I learned...

DATE ___/___/___

Allah, forgive me for the bad things I've done or said, even the ones nobody else knows about but You and I.

I make dua for...

_____
_____
_____
_____

Islam goals I am working on are...

_____
_____
_____
_____

One thing I wish I did differently to make today even better was...

_____
_____
_____
_____

Today's happy moments were...

I am grateful for...

Today I learned...

DATE ___/___/___

Allah, when I am feeling sad, remind me that
Your love for me is greater than my disappointments.

I make dua for...

_____
_____
_____
_____

Islam goals I am working on are...

_____
_____
_____
_____

One thing I wish I did differently to make today even better was...

_____
_____
_____
_____

Today's happy moments were...

I am grateful for...

Today I learned...

DATE ___/___/___

Allah, make the best of my life the end of it,
the best of my actions the last of them,
the best of my days the day in which I meet You.
I make dua for...

_____

_____

_____

_____

Islam goals I am working on are...

_____

_____

_____

_____

One thing I wish I did differently to make today even better was...

_____

_____

_____

_____

Today's happy moments were...

I am grateful for...

Today I learned...

DATE ___/___/___

Allah, make my inside better than my outside.
Make my outside good as well.

I make dua for...

_____
_____
_____
_____

Islam goals I am working on are...

_____
_____
_____
_____

One thing I wish I did differently to make today even better was...

_____
_____
_____

Today's happy moments were...

I am grateful for...

Today I learned...

DATE ___/___/___

Allah, help me forgive those who mistreated me,
forget the bad things that have happened to me,
and find peace and joy in reading and listening to the Quran.
I make dua for...

_____
_____
_____
_____

Islam goals I am working on are...

_____
_____
_____
_____

One thing I wish I did differently to make today even better was...

_____
_____
_____
_____

Today's happy moments were...

I am grateful for...

Today I learned...

DATE ___/___/___

Allah, help me always remember You,
throughout the day, through big tasks and small.

I make dua for...

_____

_____

_____

_____

Islam goals I am working on are...

_____

_____

_____

_____

One thing I wish I did differently to make today even better was...

_____

_____

_____

Today's happy moments were...

I am grateful for...

Today I learned...

DATE ___/___/___

Allah, I ask that You lead me to good.
I ask that I have complete trust in You.
I ask that I have good thoughts of You.
I make dua for...

___

Islam goals I am working on are...

___

One thing I wish I did differently to make today even better was...

___

Today's happy moments were...

I am grateful for...

Today I learned...

DATE ___/___/___

Allah, give me happiness in whatever You gave me, and do not let me be attached to something which You have turned away from me.
I make dua for...

_____
_____
_____
_____

Islam goals I am working on are...

_____
_____
_____
_____

One thing I wish I did differently to make today even better was...

_____
_____
_____

Today's happy moments were...

I am grateful for...

Today I learned...

DATE ___/___/___

Allah, I ask for everything that
Your Prophet Muhammad ﷺ asked for.

I make dua for...

_____
_____
_____
_____

Islam goals I am working on are...

_____
_____
_____
_____

One thing I wish I did differently to make today even better was...

_____
_____
_____
_____

Today's happy moments were...

I am grateful for...

Today I learned...

DATE ___/___/___

Allah, make me a humble person and protect me from thinking I am better than anybody else.

I make dua for...

_____
_____
_____
_____
_____

Islam goals I am working on are...

_____
_____
_____
_____

One thing I wish I did differently to make today even better was...

_____
_____
_____

Today's happy moments were...

I am grateful for...

Today I learned...

DATE ___/___/___

Allah, surround me with people I love and You love.

I make dua for...

_____
_____
_____
_____

Islam goals I am working on are...

_____
_____
_____
_____

One thing I wish I did differently to make today even better was...

_____
_____
_____
_____

Today's happy moments were...

I am grateful for...

Today I learned...

DATE ___/___/___

Allah, help me build on my strengths and keep me away from focusing too much on my weaknesses.

I make dua for...

_____
_____
_____
_____

Islam goals I am working on are...

_____
_____
_____
_____

One thing I wish I did differently to make today even better was...

_____
_____
_____

Today's happy moments were...

I am grateful for...

Today I learned...

DATE ___/___/___

Allah, help me trust that even when I do not understand them all, Your rules are good for me.

I make dua for...

_____
_____
_____
_____

Islam goals I am working on are...

_____
_____
_____
_____

One thing I wish I did differently to make today even better was...

_____
_____
_____

Today's happy moments were...

I am grateful for...

Today I learned...

DATE ___/___/___

Allah, make school enjoyable for me.

I make dua for...

_____
_____
_____
_____

Islam goals I am working on are...

_____
_____
_____
_____

One thing I wish I did differently to make today even better was...

_____
_____
_____

Today's happy moments were...

I am grateful for...

Today I learned...

DATE ___/___/___

Allah, protect me from illnesses that cause too much pain and for too long.

I make dua for...

___

___

___

___

Islam goals I am working on are...

___

___

___

___

One thing I wish I did differently to make today even better was...

___

___

___

Today's happy moments were...

I am grateful for...

Today I learned...

DATE ___/___/___

Allah, make me accepting of people with different backgrounds. And make it easy for everyone else to accept me the way I am. I make dua for...

_____
_____
_____
_____

Islam goals I am working on are...

_____
_____
_____
_____

One thing I wish I did differently to make today even better was...

_____
_____
_____
_____

Today's happy moments were...

I am grateful for...

Today I learned...

DATE ___/___/___

Allah, give peace to the world. Protect the people who are going through war and natural disasters. Protect us from living in fear and hardships.
I make dua for...

___

___

___

___

Islam goals I am working on are...

___

___

___

___

One thing I wish I did differently to make today even better was...

___

___

___

Today's happy moments were...

I am grateful for...

Today I learned...

DATE ___/___/___

Allah, make enjoyable for me the actions that bring me closer to You and Your love.

I make dua for...

_____
_____
_____
_____

Islam goals I am working on are...

_____
_____
_____
_____

One thing I wish I did differently to make today even better was...

_____
_____
_____

Today's happy moments were...

I am grateful for...

Today I learned...

DATE ___/___/___

Allah, make me a wise and smart person. Make me the kind of person that works hard to figure things out.

I make dua for...

_____
_____
_____
_____

Islam goals I am working on are...

_____
_____
_____
_____

One thing I wish I did differently to make today even better was...

_____
_____
_____
_____

Today's happy moments were...

I am grateful for...

Today I learned...

DATE ___/___/___

Allah, You made me the way I am. All of your creations are beautiful, so protect me from thinking badly about myself: how I am, how I do, or how I look.

I make dua for...

_____
_____
_____
_____

Islam goals I am working on are...

_____
_____
_____
_____

One thing I wish I did differently to make today even better was...

_____
_____
_____
_____

Today's happy moments were...

I am grateful for...

Today I learned...

DATE ___/___/___

Allah, help me stay away from things that are bad for me even when it is hard.

I make dua for...

_____
_____
_____
_____

Islam goals I am working on are...

_____
_____
_____
_____

One thing I wish I did differently to make today even better was...

_____
_____
_____

Today's happy moments were...

I am grateful for...

Today I learned...

DATE ___/___/___

Allah, safeguard me with Islam while I am standing.
Safeguard me with Islam while I am sitting.
Safeguard me with Islam while I am lying down.
I make dua for...

_____
_____
_____
_____

Islam goals I am working on are...

_____
_____
_____
_____

One thing I wish I did differently to make today even better was...

_____
_____
_____
_____

Today's happy moments were...

I am grateful for...

Today I learned...

DATE ___/___/___

Allah, I ask You for Paradise and
all that would draw me closer to it.
Be it by the words I speak or actions I perform.
I make dua for...

_____

_____

_____

_____

Islam goals I am working on are...

_____

_____

_____

_____

One thing I wish I did differently to make today even better was...

_____

_____

_____

Today's happy moments were...

I am grateful for...

Today I learned...

DATE __/__/__

Allah, I ask You to protect all my Muslim brothers and sisters.

I make dua for...

___

___

___

___

Islam goals I am working on are...

___

___

___

___

One thing I wish I did differently to make today even better was...

___

___

___

___

Today's happy moments were...

I am grateful for...

Today I learned...

DATE ___/___/___

Allah, give barakah to my parents' time so they have more time to spend with me. Make our time together enjoyable for all of us.
I make dua for...

___

Islam goals I am working on are...

___

One thing I wish I did differently to make today even better was...

Today's happy moments were...

I am grateful for...

Today I learned...

DATE ___/___/___

Allah, give us the good of this life
and the good of the afterlife.

I make dua for...

_____
_____
_____
_____

Islam goals I am working on are...

_____
_____
_____
_____

One thing I wish I did differently to make today even better was...

_____
_____
_____
_____

Today's happy moments were...

I am grateful for...

Today I learned...

DATE ___/___/___

Allah, have mercy on my parents as they brought me up when I was small.

I make dua for...

_____
_____
_____
_____

Islam goals I am working on are...

_____
_____
_____
_____

One thing I wish I did differently to make today even better was...

_____
_____
_____
_____

Today's happy moments were...

I am grateful for...

Today I learned...

DATE ___/___/___

Allah, make me one who delivers on the five pillars of Islam.

I make dua for...

_____
_____
_____
_____

Islam goals I am working on are...

_____
_____
_____
_____

One thing I wish I did differently to make today even better was...

_____
_____
_____

Today's happy moments were...

I am grateful for...

Today I learned...

DATE ___/___/___

Allah, protect me from lack of courage, from laziness, from cowardice, from mental illness, and from having debts.

I make dua for...

_____
_____
_____
_____

Islam goals I am working on are...

_____
_____
_____
_____

One thing I wish I did differently to make today even better was...

_____
_____
_____

Today's happy moments were...

I am grateful for...

Today I learned...

DATE ___/___/___

Allah, protect me from too much worry and from sadness.

I make dua for...

_____
_____
_____
_____

Islam goals I am working on are...

_____
_____
_____
_____

One thing I wish I did differently to make today even better was...

_____
_____
_____
_____

Today's happy moments were...

I am grateful for...

Today I learned...

DATE ___/___/___

Allah, make me fearful of You and obedient to You.

I make dua for...

_____
_____
_____
_____

Islam goals I am working on are...

_____
_____
_____
_____

One thing I wish I did differently to make today even better was...

_____
_____
_____

Today's happy moments were...

I am grateful for...

Today I learned...

DATE ___/___/___

Allah, create love among our hearts
and show us the paths of peace.

I make dua for...

_____
_____
_____
_____

Islam goals I am working on are...

_____
_____
_____
_____

One thing I wish I did differently to make today even better was...

_____
_____
_____

Today's happy moments were...

I am grateful for...

Today I learned...

DATE ___/___/___

By filling out The Dua Journal, I learned...

Some duas that were answered: